The Minnesota Cabin Planning Guide & Workbook

By Kimberly M. Hanlon

The Minnesota Cabin Planning Guide and Workbook

Published by
Propitious Publishing, Inc.
310 4th Avenue South
Suite 5010
Minneapolis, Minnesota 55415

ISBN: 9780985933708 (PDF)
ISBN: 9780985933715 (Paperback)

Table of Contents

Introduction   **1**

Chapter 1 – How Cabins Are Owned and Passed   **6**
Down - *Where Real Estate Law and Inheritance*
Law Intersect
     How Cabins Are Owned
         Fee Simple
         Tenants in Common
         Joint Tenancy
     How Cabins Are Passed Down
         Without a Plan
         With a Will
         Through a Transfer on Death Deed
         Through a Trust

Chapter 2 – What's the Worst that Can Hap-   **20**
pen? *The All Too Common Scenarios*
     The Lingering Ex
     The Spendthrift
     The Cabin Hog
     The Cheapskates
     The Railroader
     The Hoarder

Chapter 3 – Getting the Lay of the Land - *What*   **37**
Your Planning Options Are Under the Law
     Cabin Co-Ownership Agreement
     Cabin LLC
     Cabin Trusts
         The Garden Variety
         The Tax Strategy Plan
         The Dynasty Plan

Chapter 4 – What's Ideal and What's Real – *Ask-*   **49**
ing the Right Questions and Dealing with the
Real Answers
      About Owning the Cabin
      About Using the Cabin
      About Paying For the Cabin
      About Managing the Cabin

Chapter 5 - Making a Plan to Keep the Peace –   **61**
Choosing the Right Planning Option for Your
Situation and Your Goals
      The Process of Planning
      Considering Your Larger Plan
      Making the Right Choice

Chapter 6 – Getting It Done – *What's Next and*   **74**
What to Expect
      What's Next?
      About Choosing your Attorney
      So, How Much Is All This Going to Cost?
      How Long Is This Going to Take?
      My Final Words

About the Author   **84**

Introduction

Cabins aren't like other assets you own and treating them just like any other asset in your estate plan really doesn't work. If you think about it, unless you own a family business that you expect to pass down to your kids, your kids don't expect to each share and use your house, your cars, your things like your furniture and such, and any monetary assets you leave behind will be divided and distributed. What's likely to happen with your house and cars and other stuff is that it will be sold and the proceeds will be divided and distributed.

That's not what most people want to have happen with their cabin – usually they want to pass it down to their kids or grandkids to share and use – and rightfully so, they've had years of creating great memories in that cabin – it's been the family's haven for tranquility and everyone thinks of it as a place of happiness. Who wouldn't want that to continue?

In an ideal world, you would give the cabin to your kids and they would naturally work out among themselves who was going to be there when, how the bills were going to get paid, and how the upkeep was going to be managed. Perhaps your kids can and will do just that. But what about the next generation? Cousins rarely have the closeness of siblings, and there's likely to be more of them. So even if you think your kids can manage it without planning, the cabin tranquility is still likely to be short lived.

Even if your kids get along well, and even if you expect that all your grandkids will get along well, there's still some scenarios that are all too common that you should know about. Here's the biggest one: one of your kids gets divorced, and because your child owned a portion of the cabin as a tenant in common, a portion of their share was awarded to their now ex-spouse.

One of the rules about tenants in common is that every person who owns a piece of the property has the right to use it as much as they like, so that ex-spouse has the right to use the cabin all the time, any time, and bring his or her new spouse and step-kids, too. If that doesn't create family tension, I don't know what will. If you think the chance of *this* happening in your family is remote, consider how many people you know who are divorced and re-married.

Even if your family all gets along, and ex-spouses with new spouses in the mix won't be a problem, here's another scenario to think about – If one of your kids or grandkids gets into financial hot water and either files for bankruptcy or gets a judgment against them, their interest in the cabin can be used to pay those creditors. Because a cabin is not a homestead, a judgment creditor can force the property into foreclosure, then it's an issue that everyone has to deal with. If you think the chance of *this* is remote, consider how many people you know who have had financial struggles at some point in their lives.

So, let's say that your family is exceptional, and everyone gets along and will continue to get along, even with ex-spouses and their new spouses, and no one will file for bankruptcy or get a judgment against them, there's still the garden variety cabin issues that can create conflict.

Issues like when one person uses the cabin more than the others but isn't contributing towards upkeep and expenses, or when one person isn't using the cabin at all and so they don't think they should have to contribute anything, or when someone thinks it's time to redecorate but the others don't agree, or they think the one redecorating has bad taste. Or when one person thinks the cabin is a good place to store a bunch of stuff and no one else wants to look at the other person's things piled up here and there.

There's a ton of small (and not so small) disagreements that can arise when people have shared use and shared responsibility for a property without some system in place establishing rules and how decisions are going to be made.

So, when the conflict arises and someone wants out of the cabin and the others still want in, what happens? If they can't come to an agreement to buy out the one who wants to sell, then that person can go to court and file a special lawsuit that's called an *action for partition*.

What that means is that they are asking the court to order that the property be sold and that they be given their share of the proceeds based on the percentage of the property that they own. And you know what – the order will be granted. The judge doesn't care that the cabin means so much to your family or that there's a rich history of happy memories there. The judge applies the law and the law says that a tenant in common can force the sale of the property.

What's more, the attorney's fees and costs of bringing this lawsuit, which will not be cheap by any means, will come from the proceeds of the sale of the cabin. Which means that for the ones who wanted to keep the cabin, but couldn't afford to buy out the one who wanted out, they are both losing the cabin and paying a portion of the legal costs that made them lose the cabin.

It's no wonder that family members stop talking after this sort of lawsuit. Sometimes they don't talk for years.

Sometimes they don't ever talk again.

That may sound bleak to you, but it happens all too often. It doesn't have to be that way.

With some advanced planning, you can create the systems that establish rules and determine how decisions will be made, and you can decide who will provide the leadership for those decisions. You can make the system legally binding so that you know the system will work when your family needs it to. You can even build in protection from creditors and ex-spouses. If you really want to have the cabin be a haven of tranquility for generations to come, you can provide funding for the upkeep and expenses.

You can only do this, though, with some forethought.

Many families are lost when it comes to thinking through all the things they need to consider and they really don't know what their options are regarding the law. That's why I wrote the Minnesota Cabin Planning Guide & Workbook. It's designed to let you know about the scenarios you will want to watch out for, let you know what your options are based on your situation and goals, ask the questions you don't know needed to be answered, and provide some guidance on exploring what the answers might look like for your family.

Remember that every family is different, so no two cabin plans are just alike. That doesn't mean it has to be hard or complicated, though. The Minnesota Cabin Planning Guide & Workbook makes it simple, and provides the start of what you'll need to work with your attorney in creating the plan that is just right for your family.

Chapter 1

How Cabins Are Owned and Passed Down

Where Real Estate Law and Inheritance Law Intersect

How Cabins Are Owned

A cabin can be owned in a number of ways, and how a cabin is owned will be found on the Title to the property. There are more ways a property can be owned than the three that I talk about in this guide, but these three cover the vast majority of cases out there. If, when you look at the title to your cabin's property, you cannot figure out which one applies in your case or you think your cabin may be owned in one of the other ways I didn't list here, but would like to know what it means, give me a call and we'll sort it out for you.

Fee Simple

Fee Simple simply means that a single person (or entity, in the case of a Trust or a Company) owns the cabin. Keep in mind, however, that if you own your cabin by yourself in Fee Simple and you're married, your spouse may have property rights to the cabin, either through the family law (divorce) rules or through the probate (inheritance) rules. Determining what your spouse's rights may be to your cabin is based on your specific circumstances, so if you own your cabin in fee simple but are married and want to know what rights your spouse may have, if any, then you'll need to give me a call or ask your attorney.

Tenants in Common

When a property is owned by more than one person (or entity), it is owned in tenancy. In Minnesota, we have *tenancy in common* and *joint tenancy*. In some other states, there is *tenancy in the entirety*, which is a name for joint tenancy for a married couple.

When property is owned by more than one person, the default form that the property is titled in is tenancy in common, unless joint tenancy is specifically written on the title. In tenancy in common, an owner's share of the property passes to the person or people they direct in their estate plan, or if they haven't made a plan, by their heirs under the probate laws.

As tenants in common, the owners can have unequal ownership shares, but they each have complete right to use the property as though they owned it alone. In terms of cabins, that means that by two or three generations, a cabin could be owned by a dozen people, but without legal planning to manage the property, all of them would have the right to use the cabin all day, every day. It can be problematic getting someone to leave when they have the right to be there, and it can be problematic to prevent someone from using the cabin when they have the right to be there.

When there are multiple owners as tenants in common, any single owner can sell their ownership share to anyone they want unless there is a legally binding agreement that prevents them from doing so. Imagine owning a part of a cabin with people you know, and then someone decides to sell their share, and suddenly you are sharing a property with a stranger!

If a tenant in common doesn't want to own his or her share in the cabin anymore but cannot get anyone to buy him or her out, the one who wants out can bring a special lawsuit called an action for partition to ask the court to order that the property be sold. When the property is sold, each owner will be given their proportionate share of the proceeds based on their ownership percentage. In an action for partition, the legal fees and costs are paid out of the proceeds of the sale of the cabin, so every co-owner is contributing to the legal costs – even those who didn't want to sell or take part in the lawsuit.

An action for partition will not be inexpensive, and bringing the lawsuit can tear a family apart. The ones who want out of the cabin have their own valid reasons for wanting out and resent having to force a lawsuit to get out; and the ones who want to retain the cabin resent having to be forced to sell, and resent being forced to foot the bill for part of the legal fees.

Joint Tenancy

You may have heard of joint tenancy as "joint tenancy with right of survivorship." Whether or not the words "with right of survivorship" appear on your title, joint tenancy always means with right of survivorship.

Right of survivorship means that when one co-owner dies, their share of the cabin passes to the other co-owners. For that reason, a co-owner cannot leave their share of the cabin through their estate plan. The last co-owner to survive will then own the cabin in fee simple.

Unlike tenants in common, joint tenants must always own equal shares in the cabin. When there are four joint tenants, each one owns 25% of the property. When one of them dies, the remaining three each own 33 1/3% of the property.

If one joint tenant sells their share of the cabin to someone else, that breaks the joint tenancy and the result is that the new ownership will be as tenants in common, unless they all specifically elect to be joint tenants on the new title.

Like tenants in common, joint tenants each have complete right to use the property as though they owned it alone, so you can encounter the same types of issues with someone not leaving or being able to prevent someone from using it. Unlike with tenancy in common, where the number of owners tends to multiply as time goes on, increasing the likelihood of conflict, joint tenancy has the opposite effect.

If you start with a small number of joint tenants who all get along, the likelihood of conflict increasing is more remote (although not inconceivable) and the number of people to engage in a conflict will eventually dwindle until there is a sole owner.

Note that joint tenants don't get the benefit of a step up in *basis* (meaning that they take the property with the base value being what it was purchased for and paying capital gains tax on the full value of the property when it is sold).

How Cabins Are Passed Down

Let's take a look at the ways that your interest in your cabin, whether you own it alone or with co-owners, can be passed down to your family – provided, of course, that it isn't titled in joint tenancy.

Without a Plan

If you haven't made an estate plan, the state has made one for you. The question is, is it a plan you want?

Exactly how your estate's distribution would play out depends on the makeup of your family - whether or not you are married when you die, whether or not you have children (or if they have children), whether or not you have kids from a previous relationship, and so on.

It's not my intent to bore you with the law for every possible distribution, so I'm only going to cover a few common situations in the most general terms. To really know what the distribution would be for your estate, as it stands, without an estate plan, you should give us a call or talk with your attorney.

Here is a breakdown of the most common situations when someone dies without an estate plan:

Makeup of Your Family	Who Gets How Much
You are single, no children	Your parents get all; if no parents, then your siblings; and so on. . .
You are single, with children	All to your children (or their children if a child died before you).
You are married, no children or your and your spouse's only children are the both of yours	All to your spouse.
You are married, and either you or your spouse have children from another relationship	Your spouse gets the first $150,000 plus ½ of the balance of the estate; the other ½ goes to your children, or if no children, to your parents, and so on . . .

Your spouse, if you have one, can also take a share of your non-probate assets (like life insurance proceeds and retirement accounts) based on the length of your marriage. Your spouse also has some other rights, like a right to a family allowance, a right to live in the homestead house until he or she dies, and rights relating to wages and retirement benefits. This is not a complete list of the rights surviving spouses have in Minnesota, but this includes the main ones.

When you die without an estate plan, the court has no choice but to apply the law. If you want something other than the plan the state has made for you, then you must do some estate planning.

If your cabin passes to multiple people, the new owners will be tenants in common.

With a Will

When you make a will, you get to decide who gets what (with a few exceptions I'll cover in a moment), who is going to be your personal representative (the person who manages your estate before the court), who will be guardian of your minor children, and what your final wishes are for your remains.

You can choose to leave your property in unequal amounts to different people, designate certain specific items or property to go to specific people, leave some to charities, and you can choose to exclude people that you don't want to leave anything to. Here's the exception, though – you cannot exclude your spouse without their consent. Remember – your spouse has a bucket of rights under the law, and they can waive those rights with a prenuptial or post-nuptial agreement or through consent documents, but otherwise they have the right to take at minimum their share that is allotted under the law. Likewise, your minor children have rights to family allowance for maintenance if your spouse doesn't survive you.

Sometimes people are surprised that you can disinherit your kids, but you can't disinherit your spouse without their consent. If you do want to disinherit your kids, it's important that you do so explicitly in your will, otherwise it could be challenged. If you have made a will and later had a child, that child can have certain rights to a share of your estate as an omitted heir, depending on the circumstances.

If you are leaving your cabin to more than one person in your will, you can designate whether they are getting the cabin as tenants in common (in which case you could make unequal distributions if you chose) or as joint tenants (in which case every person gets an equal share). If you just give your interest in the cabin but don't say anything about how the new ownership will be titled, then the default is that they will be tenants in common.

People sometimes think that a will is all they need for cabin planning, and if all you want to do is transfer your interest in the cabin to the people or organizations you choose, then you might be right. However, if you want to avoid any of the situations we'll talk about in Chapter 2 (**What's the Worst that Can Happen?** *The All Too Common Scenarios*), then a Will just won't do.

Through a Transfer on Death Deed

A transfer on death deed is a relatively recent legal development and has some aspects of real estate law and some aspects of estate planning law. Sometimes people want to transfer their real estate to their children through a *quit claim deed* to avoid probate or to get their house out of their asset portfolio for a number of reasons. The problem with using a quit claim deed is that the transfer is immediate and permanent – there is no going back and changing your mind later.

This can become an issue if your relationship with the people you transfer your real estate to starts to change, or if they have creditors that will put a lien on the property or even foreclose on it. You could be ousted in ways you can't imagine when you least expect it. Not to mention that your cost basis transfers to your children when you gift them your property while you live, so they will be stuck with the capital gains tax bill when they sell it.

The transfer on death deed was developed as a safer alternative to using a quit claim deed when you want to transfer your real estate to avoid probate, but you also want to continue to use your property until you die.

Using a transfer on death deed, you can change your mind and revoke it – just like a Will – because you haven't actually made the transfer yet. The property only transfers once you die. Because the property hasn't transferred yet and you retain the ability to change your mind, your kids' creditors cannot place a lien on your property or foreclose on it, and your kids can't kick you out of the property if your relationship with them falters.

Transfer on death deeds are most commonly used in small estates as a part of a probate avoidance plan, without using a trust. Although that is its common use, there is no reason that a transfer on death deed could not be used to transfer ownership of your cabin after you die, outside of your other estate planning efforts.

Much like what you can do with a Will, if all you want to do is transfer your interest in the cabin to the people or organizations you choose, then a transfer on death deed may be a good choice for you. However, if you want to avoid any of the situations we'll talk about in Chapter 2 (**What's the Worst that Can Happen?** *The All Too Common Scenarios*), then a transfer on death deed isn't a good choice.

Through a Trust

I find that people sometimes have a hard time wrapping their minds around how trusts work, primarily because a trust isn't a physical thing that you can point to in the world, other than the piece of paper that it's written on. It's a conceptual thing, created solely in language, and it's much harder to keep a new concept held in your mind than it is to keep an image of something concrete in your mind.

If I say the word "lamp", the image that comes to your mind might be different than the image that comes to my mind, but we both have an image of something that holds a lightbulb and illuminates a room. If I say the word "trust", you might picture *Gilligan Island's* Thurston Howell III or you might picture something else, but whatever it is, it won't actually be a picture of a trust.

People understand trusts better when I analogize them to something that is concrete in the world, something they can picture in their minds.

A trust is like a box. A box is designed to hold stuff, and so are trusts. A trust is a legal entity that is created to hold property for the benefit of someone else. The person who puts the property into the trust is called the grantor (or also called the settlor), the person who benefits from the trust is called the beneficiary, and the person who manages the property while it's in the trust is called the trustee. Often, the grantor is also the initial trustee and the first beneficiary. That's why it's possible to have everything you own be in a trust, but your day to day life won't feel any different.

Imagine that everything you own fits into a box. There's a type of trust in which you can reach into the box and pull anything you like out, or even take everything out and throw away the box. That's a *revocable trust*.

Imagine that the box with your stuff in it has a lid on it. Now you can't reach in and take the stuff out. That's an *irrevocable trust*.

There's a rule about trusts that says that if you have the power to reach in and take something out, then your creditors (and Uncle Sam) have the power to compel you to take stuff out to satisfy your obligation to them. If you don't have that power, they cannot use what's in the trust for your obligations. That's why we use irrevocable trusts to provide protection from estate taxes, creditors, and future ex-spouses.

I'm talking about this in general, broad terms. There are many, many different types of revocable and irrevocable trusts with differing rules for differing purposes.

Whatever property you put in your trust is owned by the trust, and no longer owned by you personally. When you die, that property is not included in your probate estate because it wasn't owned by you. If you want to avoid having your estate be a matter of public record, and letting people know what you own, what you owe, and what your are leaving to whom and how much, then trust planning can achieve your goal.

The purpose of the probate court is to provide a legal mechanism for transferring property from a person who has died to the person who is getting the property next. A dead person can't sign a deed, so there has to be some other legal mechanism to make that happen. In a trust, the trustee has the authority to sign the deed, and if the trustee dies, there's a way to select a successor trustee, so in theory, there will always be someone available to sign the deed. That is why a trust creates a legal mechanism for transferring property outside of the court process.

Like I mentioned earlier, a trust is created solely in language for a particular purpose. Different trusts with different purposes have different language. It's the language that is chosen in creating the trust that determines what the rules for that trust will be – who the grantor is, what powers they are retaining, and the purpose of the trust; who the trustee will be, what powers and obligations they will have, and how they will be replaced; who the beneficiaries are, what benefits they get and under what conditions, and the powers they may have; how long the trust may last, how it may come to an end, and what happens when it does end. Trusts can be highly specific with customized rules. They can be very personalized.

Unlike with any of the other estate planning tools we've talked about, with a trust you can direct how the property is used, or not used, or when it is used, and who can or cannot use it.

For that reason, how property is passed down in a trust is dependent on the language that created that particular trust. Generally speaking, the grantor transfers the property in the trust, the trustee manages the property and then distributes the property to the beneficiaries according to the rules of that trust.

Chapter 2

What's the Worst that Can Happen?

The All Too Common Scenarios

I've encountered plenty of people who have inherited their parents' cabin without a cabin plan and who have had family relationships damaged, sometimes irreparably, over the fallout from the ensuing disagreements. What follows are the all-too-common scenarios that unfold when there's no plan in place to prevent family discord, protect relationships, and provide for structure and decision-making.

The Lingering Ex

Tom, Peter, and Beth were siblings who inherited their parents' cabin in equal shares. Tom was married to Linda and they had two boys; Peter was married to Carrie and they had one daughter; and Beth was married to Roger and they had two kids, a boy and a girl. Tom and Peter were always polite to Roger, but they didn't particularly like him. When he wasn't around, Beth was livelier, laughed more, and seemed more free and at ease. When Roger was around, she was more reserved and didn't seem as free to be herself or voice her opinion. They had never seen Roger be abusive to Beth, or anything like that, but he didn't seem to mesh well with the rest of the family. Linda and Carrie thought Roger could be a bit controlling at times, and he sometimes said things that were bordering on rude to their kids.

When Beth told the family that she was going to leave Roger, everyone was supportive and perhaps even a bit relieved. Beth and Roger went through a divorce, and in the court process Roger ended up with part of Beth's share of the family cabin. Beth didn't think it was a big deal at the time because Roger said that he would sell the cabin interest back to her when she was back on her feet after the divorce and he said he would be glad to give her all the time she needed.

The next summer, Peter and Linda were up at the cabin with the boys when Roger pulled up in his pickup truck with two jet skis in tow. He had come for the weekend with his new girlfriend and her two kids. Peter and Linda were upset because it occurred to them that Roger wasn't a part of the family anymore, was crashing their weekend uninvited, and was totally out of line to presume he could use the cabin – let alone with a new girlfriend.

Angry words were exchanged. Roger ended up leaving, but not before threating to sue Peter and Linda for forcing him out of the cabin he owned and had every right to use.

On Monday, Peter talked to Beth and learned that Roger did, in fact, own part of the cabin. She was shocked to hear about the exchange that took place over the weekend; Peter was shocked to learn that Roger shared ownership of the cabin with the rest of the family.

Peter and Tom, when they realized that Roger had as much right to be at the cabin as they did, determined that they would buy Roger out. When they approached Roger about it, he said that he would sell his part of the cabin to them and the price he quoted was three times what the value had been calculated to be during the divorce process. Roger stated that otherwise he didn't want to sell because he always liked being at the cabin, he wanted to keep using it with the kids, and keeping this one was much cheaper than getting one himself.

Peter and Tom consulted an attorney and found out that under the circumstances, their options were to buy Roger out under agreed upon negotiated terms, or let Roger use the cabin as was his right, or bring an action for partition to ask the court order that the property be sold for fair market value and the proceeds of the sale be distributed to the owners in their respective shares. Since they wanted to keep the cabin, but they didn't want to share it with Roger and whomever he might bring around, they decided to pony up and buy him out at a premium. Peter and Tom tried to get financing using their own homes as collateral, but they couldn't get a bank to approve them for the purchase.

They waited to see if the situation with Roger wanting to use the cabin would go away, but it didn't. Even if they worked out in advance who was going to be using the cabin on which days so they didn't have to run into him, they didn't like the idea of his being around and using their stuff and they didn't like the idea of strangers being brought into their second home. Ultimately, they ended up bringing the action for partition and selling the cabin.

That altered the relationship between Beth and her brothers for a number of years. Beth felt badly that her brothers had to lose the cabin they all loved and she thought they were angry at her for allowing Roger to get ownership in the cabin in the divorce. Tom and Peter felt a rift with Beth because they had gone through extraordinary measures to try to keep the cabin within the family, but she never acknowledged them for their effort. They didn't blame Beth for their losing the cabin – they blamed Roger – but nonetheless it impacted the family relationship for some time. And, of course, everyone was sad to let go of the cabin.

The Spendthrift

Mark and Robin were siblings who inherited their parents' cabin. Mark and his wife Cindy never seemed to have enough money, despite Mark having a good job with a steady income and Cindy working part-time while the kids were in school. Robin was in a long term relationship with Steve, but they never married. She was independent and career focused, and she lived modestly for her income.

Mark, Cindy, Robin and Steve had no issues sharing the cabin. Some weekends they would all be there at once; sometimes it was just Mark, Cindy, and the kids; and sometimes it was just Robin and Steve. When it came time to pay the utility bills and property taxes on the cabin, Robin would pay for it and eventually Mark would pay her back, in dribbles and drabs here and there. Robin never worried about it because she had plenty in savings and she knew that

Mark had a lot of financial responsibilities with his family. The expenses for the cabin weren't an enormous amount – certainly not worth fighting over.

Over time, Mark and Cindy's debts got out of control. They started getting sued by credit card companies and they were behind on their home mortgage, very close to foreclosure. When they were about to get the first default judgment from a creditor, they decided to file for Chapter 7 bankruptcy. Mark's half of the cabin didn't fit within the exemption amount after all the other assets he and Cindy were trying to hold onto, so Mark's half of the cabin was included in his bankruptcy estate and had to be sold. Of course, the only viable buyer for Mark's half had to be Robin, or else the cabin would have to be put up for sale.

While Robin did have some savings and she did have good credit, she neither wanted to wipe out her savings to buy Mark's half of the cabin nor did she want to take a mortgage out on the cabin and add that payment to her own monthly expenses. She liked it that she shared her parents' cabin with her brother, but she didn't want to have to pay for everything all the time.

They ended up selling the cabin to satisfy Mark's creditors.

The Cabin Hog

Matt, Patty, and Tim inherited their parents' cabin. Matt lived closest to the cabin and liked to use it with his family as a summer retreat and as a hunting lodge in hunting season. Patty and her family were a few hours' drive away from the cabin, so it was less convenient for them to use it frequently. Tim had taken a job in San Francisco, California, and only returned to Minnesota for a visit every few years.

One year, Tim came to visit Minnesota for the last week in June and the first week in July. While he was in Minnesota, Tim planned to get together with a bunch of friends from college who had stayed in the area. Tim told Matt that he was going to use the cabin for the Fourth of July weekend to host his reunion, and Matt told Tim that he couldn't use it because Matt's family already had plans to be there.

Tim was very upset and told Matt that he was being unreasonable, that Matt had unfettered use of the cabin for the past four years and Tim hadn't used it at all, so the one time he wanted to use it he should be able to use it! Matt was very upset, as well, and told his brother that he could use the cabin anytime he liked, he just had to let them know and they would be glad to let him have it, but his not using the cabin was his own choice, had nothing to do with the holiday weekend, and that his family's plans shouldn't be disrupted simply because Tim hadn't been to the cabin for so long.

Tim ended up hosting his reunion at a restaurant. After he flew back to San Francisco, he called Matt and told him that he wanted out of the cabin. Matt said that seemed a bit extreme and told Tim that he didn't want to buy him out because he didn't need more ownership than what he had – he was content with the status quo. Tim then called Patty to see if she wanted to buy him out, which of course, she didn't want to because she didn't need more ownership in the cabin, especially with as infrequently as she used it.

Tim brought an action for partition, but before the judge could order that the property be sold, the siblings settled in mediation. Matt bought half and Patty bought half of Tim's shares at a very reasonable price. All three, however, resented the legal costs.

Tim and Matt didn't speak until years later at Patty's youngest daughter's wedding.

The Cheapskate

Bill, Frank, and Marty inherited their parents' cabin. Bill was an outdoorsman and like to hunt and fish, plus he would take any chance he had to get out of the city that he could. Even before their dad passed, Bill spent time at the cabin regularly. Frank traveled a lot for his work, so when he was in Minnesota, his favorite place to be was his own home, although he did enjoy going to the cabin every now and then, especially for a long holiday weekend. Marty lived in Boston and had his own busy life on the east coast, so he had never even set foot in the cabin since his sophomore year in college.

Bill was a good carpenter and could do better handyman work than the average person you might hire, and he enjoyed tinkering and fixing things. Bill had done the upkeep on the cabin and their dad's house while his health was in decline. When the boys inherited the cabin, Bill continued to do all the maintenance on the cabin, which worked out because he spent so much time there.

When the property tax bill came due, Bill sent an email to his brothers letting them know how much the total was and he included the list of utility bill payments he had made that season and let them know that he had replaced the water valve at the pump because it had become cracked over the freeze/thaw winter cycle. The bill for the materials was nominal, but the total for the utilities and property tax was not insignificant. He said he would appreciate their payment within the month.

Frank thought it was fair that the cabin bills be split evenly between the owners, but Marty saw things differently. Marty wrote back to Bill and said he didn't see the point in paying for a cabin that he was never, ever going to use. He especially didn't see that he should be paying for utilities when the only person who was being kept comfortable by them was Bill. Marty thought if he should pay anything, it should only be a small fraction of the property tax. After all, he wasn't the one using the cabin and wearing it out.

Bill was not only rather offended by the idea that Marty just accused him of being a freeloader, he was infuriated that Marty never acknowledged the time that Bill had put into maintaining the cabin, which would need to be done whether anyone used it or not.

Bill responded that each of them had a share in the property value in the cabin, and the amount of equity in the cabin would continue to grow, and that it was not right for Marty's equity value to grow just as much as Bill's, but for Bill to pay more in tax and expenses just because he was there to use the cabin whereas Marty was not. He also pointed out that maintenance regularly needed to be done on the cabin from time and the elements, and not necessarily from use, and that it wasn't right for Bill to pay more for expenses just because he was there to use the cabin whereas Marty was not. Lastly, he said that he had actually saved everyone a lot of money by doing the labor on the valve replacement himself, and that if he had thought of it before, he would have considered what that time was worth if they had hired a handyman to do the job. Plus, he pointed out, he may be the one mostly using the cabin, but he was also the one who was mostly maintaining the cabin, which everyone benefitted from.

Despite all of Bill's points, Marty didn't want to pay his share of a cabin that he was never going to use. Marty said that if the cabin had so much property value, that he would like his share of it now.

Bill couldn't afford to buy Marty out, but Frank could afford it, although Frank wasn't interested in owning more of a cabin that he was only going to use on holiday weekends, if that much. Bill ended up working it out for Frank to provide the financing for Bill to buy Marty's share of the cabin. Now Bill makes cabin payments to Frank, and when it comes time to pay the property taxes or expenses, Bill is responsible for 2/3 of it and Frank is responsible for 1/3 of it.

The Railroader

Tammy had always been the outspoken one in the family, so no one was ever surprised when she appointed herself as the boss for any situation that came up, and she had the expectation that everyone would agree with her and see that she was right – about everything, all the time.

That had been the family dynamic between her and her three siblings, Rick, Mary, and Donna, all through grade school, middle school, junior high, and high school. It would have continued that way through college, but they all went to different schools.

By the time the four siblings inherited their parents' cabin, they had spouses and kids of their own, their own careers and lives, and they weren't particularly close. Shortly after getting the cabin, all four met at the cabin along with their spouses to clean it up and decide what to do next. Over the weekend, Tammy took over and started to unilaterally decide what would go and what would stay. Rick's wife didn't understand why he was letting Tammy call all the shots, especially when he wasn't like that at home, and she could tell that he was not happy about how things were going down. He told his wife that it was easier to let Tammy have her way than to argue with her about it.

Mary got upset when Tammy was going to throw out the perfectly good bunk beds that she and Donna used to share as kids, and that she wanted her girls to share. When Mary told Tammy that she thought the bunk beds should stay, Tammy said "everyone agrees with me that they are too old and they are a bit ugly." Tammy then went person to person to get alignment with the idea that the bunk beds were old and ugly. By the end of the day, everyone felt like it was easier to throw out the bunk beds than hear Tammy continue to campaign against them.

After the clean-up weekend, everyone went back to their lives. A few months went by before Tammy went to the cabin with her family for the weekend. While she was there, she decided that the cabin could use some more sprucing up. She went into town and picked up new linens, new curtains, some throw pillows for the couch, and a couple of air mattresses so the cabin could sleep more people. The next Monday, she sent an email to her siblings letting them know that she had picked up some things for the cabin and that their share of the bill was $242.

Mary was livid. In truth, everyone was irritated, but Mary took it particularly personally. Mary refused to pay the bill, saying that getting all that stuff for the cabin wasn't necessary or agreed upon. She said that they should have kept the bunk beds if they wanted to accommodate more people at the cabin, and that everyone had agreed that the linens and curtains were fine as they were. The others tried to stay out of the argument, but it was hard to stay neutral when they neither wanted to have the cabin redecorated nor wanted to pay for it.

Eventually Tammy gave up on the idea of being reimbursed for her cabin purchases. Instead of making her less inclined to make unilateral decisions about the cabin, though, it made her more brazen about it. She would buy whatever she wanted whenever she wanted and make it part of the cabin. She reasoned that she wasn't getting anyone else to pay for it, and she was making the donation to the cabin for everyone's benefit, so they should be grateful for her generosity. Saint Tammy.

One weekend Rick went to the cabin with his family and his in-laws. He planned on having the kids use the air mattresses and his in-laws use the kids beds. At some point over the winter, mice had made their way into the storage cabinet where the air mattresses where stored and had nested. The air mattresses not only had holes chewed through them, they were foul and had to be thrown out. The family had to get creative about sleeping arrangements that weekend.

When Mary heard about the air mattresses being ruined by mice, it was the last straw for her. She didn't like how the cabin had changed from the simple, rustic place that she had enjoyed growing up to a decorator's hodge-podge of whatever-was-on-sale at the big box store in town. She didn't appreciate that the cabin was less usable than it had been when they started, and she didn't appreciate that when she disagreed with Tammy, Tammy would campaign against her.

Mary gave her siblings an ultimatum. It was her or Tammy, one of them had to go. Did they want to buy her out or did they want to buy Tammy out? Of course, that set Tammy off on campaigning against Mary in earnest. It spilled out to aunts, uncles, and cousins. No one was spared every horrific detail of how unreasonable Mary was being, how selfish she was after Tammy had been so generous, and on and on . . .

It took a year and a half to get the buyout negotiated and complete. Tammy ended up selling her part of the cabin to their cousin Rob who had always loved hanging out with Rick at the cabin through the years.

Tammy and Mary never spoke again, and they didn't even go to each other's children's weddings.

The Hoarder

Nancy, Virginia, and Bob were siblings and all three would have inherited Chuck and Fran's cabin, except Bob died unexpectedly of a heart attack in his late forties, so his share in the cabin was left to his wife, Jenny, instead in their wills. Jenny and Bob had been high school sweethearts and she was having a hard time moving on after he died. She didn't want to give away, throw away, or sell anything that had belonged to him, and that included large things that got in the way, like his car and his woodworking equipment.

At the same time, Jenny needed to downsize the house because she had a hard time managing the mortgage without Bob's income, and the life insurance policy he had barely covered anything past his hospital bills and funeral expenses.

Since Jenny didn't have room to store all of Bob's stuff in her smaller house, she decided to store it at the cabin. At first, Nancy and Virginia thought it would be okay. They thought it was better to let Jenny go through the grieving process at her own pace. They loved Jenny more like a sister than a sister-in-law, and they had a lot of compassion for what she was going through.

Over time, though, Bob's car wasn't being driven and it was rusting out by the side of the cabin. There wasn't an enclosed shed to put Bob's woodworking equipment in, so it was taking up space in the roofed lean-to that covered the riding lawn mower. The woodworking equipment was rusting out, and had become something like an apartment complex for critters looking to nest.

In the cabin, there was precious little drawer space and a good portion of the drawer space was taken up by Bob's old clothes, which no one was going to wear. Even Nancy's teenaged boys who could have conceivably worn them, size-wise, weren't interested in wearing their dead uncle's clothes that were so outdated.

As Nancy and Virginia's families grew and wanted to use the cabin more, Bob's stuff taking up the space became more and more of a problem. The rusted-out car was making the cabin become an eyesore, and the nesting critters in close proximity to the cabin made pest control difficult.

Nancy and Virginia eventually had enough, and told Jenny that she had to clean all of Bob's old stuff out of the cabin. Jenny was very hurt because she didn't really see that his stuff had become a problem and she didn't understand why, if it was a problem, why it was a problem now, when nothing had changed and they hadn't said anything before.

Jenny had the car towed away, since Virginia had used the word eyesore at least four times in the conversation, so it seemed to Jenny like that was the thing that was the problem.

Three months after the car was towed away, Jenny hadn't taken anything else of Bob's out, so Nancy's husband hauled the old, rusted woodworking equipment to the scrap yard one weekend. Jenny was shocked that the equipment was all gone the next time she was at the cabin – she called Nancy and Virginia to let them know the cabin had been burgled. When Nancy told her that the cabin hadn't been burgled, and that her husband had hauled Bob's woodworking equipment to the scrap yard, Jenny was outraged. She yelled at Nancy, "How could you do this without asking me?" Nancy was irate and yelled at Jenny, "Why didn't you take care of it when we asked you to over three months ago?"

Jenny felt that she wasn't welcome at the cabin anymore, which wasn't true, but that is how she felt so she stayed away. She grew distant from the family. Eventually the drawers were cleaned out and Bob's clothes made their way to the local Salvation Army. Jenny held onto her share of the cabin until she passed, and she left her share to her nieces and nephews, so the cabin ultimately stayed in the family, although the rift that it caused was never repaired.

Chapter 3

Getting the Lay of the Land

What Your Planning Options Are Under the Law

Cabin Co-Ownership Agreement

A cabin co-ownership agreement is simply a contract that all of the cabin co-owners enter into that governs the management of the cabin. Each share of the cabin is titled in the owner's name and each owner has the power to pass their shares on to whomever they wish (unless, of course, by agreement everyone has decided on some limitation in transferring shares).

These types of agreements can last a very, very long time without much trouble or they can be very, very short lived and rather delicate depending on the co-owners involved and how effectively the terms of the agreement can be managed in the real world.

When cabin co-owners pass their shares of the cabin to the next generation, the next generation take the cabin subject to and under the rules of the agreement. The current co-owners, whether that's the initial owners or subsequent generations, have the power to alter the agreement, or even agree to terminate the agreement. That's why the contract has to have terms that are effective and usable in the real world; otherwise, the owners will band together to strike down the agreement.

It's best if the owners have a certain amount of respect for each other – at least enough to follow through with their end of the bargain and enough to have faith that the others will follow through, as well. If you think about it, for this arrangement to work, everybody has to be willing to make it work.

In theory, a cabin co-ownership agreement could last in perpetuity. In reality, after a few generations there are usually too many people who have too distant a relationship to make it an effective management mechanism.

Cabin LLC

An LLC is a Limited Liability Company, a type of business entity (similar to a corporation, but not a corporation), that is organized and registered with the Secretary of State for the purpose of managing the cabin. You may wonder why someone would want to set up a company to manage a family cabin. The answers may surprise you.

An LLC is a separate legal entity in and of itself, separate from you. When an LLC has a creditor, that creditor can only look to the LLC itself for payment, and not to the owners (unless the owners have done certain things improperly that would allow the court to pierce the corporate veil). That's why it's called a *Limited Liability* company – your liability is limited to what you have put into it, but not your other personal assets.

While having the personal asset protection is a valuable thing, the real purpose of setting up a cabin LLC is to create the rules under which the cabin will operate, just like when you set up a business you set up the rules under which a business operates.

The cabin LLC operating agreement is what creates those rules, just like in a cabin co-ownership agreement. However, with a cabin LLC, if some detail is left out of the operating agreement or there is some dispute about an ambiguous term of the operating agreement, the owners (and the court, if needed) can look to the default laws that govern LLCs to see how to handle the situation. Whereas with a co-ownership agreement, the owners (and the court) have nothing but the document itself to fall back on if some issue arises that the agreement doesn't address or doesn't address adequately.

A benefit of cabin LLCs is that they can be set up to last forever, so it's a good structure if you are wanting long, long term plans, although whether or not it really does last depends on the voting that happens by future members.

Cabin Trusts

Putting your cabin into a trust as part of your estate plan isn't the same as having a cabin trust. A cabin trust is a trust specifically set up for the purpose of managing your cabin; it may have different terms than the trust in your estate plan, it may have different trustees, it may have different beneficiaries, and it possibly will have a level of detail that you never contemplated in your other trust.

The Garden Variety Plan

Unless you have a sizeable estate and need to engage in tax planning, and if you are content to have your cabin stay in the family for only a couple of generations (and then the trust ends), then a Minnesota based revocable cabin trust may be a good option for you.

Remember when we talked about a trust being like a box and that if the lid is off the box, you can reach in and take things out? That's how a revocable trust works – while you still live, you can change the terms of the trust, you can take property out of the trust, and you can even decide to not have the trust anymore. It's a good option when you don't need tax planning because it gives you flexibility and control, and you can change your mind about the terms of the trust if circumstances change.

A Minnesota-based trust can only last for up to 90 years because Minnesota is a state that has a law called "the rule against perpetuities." What this means is the trust will not be enforced past the time when a beneficiary was someone who could not be known when the trust was made (because they weren't born yet), and would not be able to be known, by the end of 21 years after the death of everyone who was alive (including children in their mother's womb but not yet born) at the time the trust was created, or 90 years, whichever is earlier. Clear as mud? It is to attorneys, too. The rule against perpetuities is one of the more difficult concepts that real estate and estate planning lawyers have to wrap our minds around. What you need to know is this: if you want your cabin plan to last more than a couple of generations, you'll need a *dynasty trust* created under the laws of a different state.

The Tax Strategy Plan

Remember when we talked about a trust being like a box, and that if the box has the lid on it, you can't take things out of it, but neither can your creditors or Uncle Sam? That's how an irrevocable trust works. When you give your property to a trust and you give up control of that property, you are taking it out of your estate completely (with a very important exception, below), and so it's not subject to estate tax (and it's not available to your creditors, either, provided you weren't making the transfer to avoid creditors).

Minnesota is one of the handful of states that has a state estate tax, in addition to the federal estate tax. The estate tax exemption for Minnesota is relatively low, and unlike the federal exemption, cannot be combined for married couples. In other words, Minnesotans need to think about tax planning at a different asset level than people in other states.

There's some good news and some bad news. The good news: there are plenty of trust planning options and strategies that help reduce or even eliminate your estate taxes. The bad news: if you are going to transfer property into your trust, then you need to file a federal gift tax return and the amount of the transfer counts towards your lifetime federal estate/gift tax exemption. In other words, to save on estate tax, Uncle Sam expects you to pay gift tax.

There are a limited number of ways around that, the most commonly used being what we call "Crummey" provisions (we know it's a funny name – it comes from a famous IRS case called Crummey vs. Commissioner of Internal Revenue). Here is how it works: every year, each person is given an annual gift tax exclusion by the IRS. It's a use it or lose it thing, but if you use it, you can give gifts up to the exclusion amount per person. If you are a married couple, you can combine your gifts and give up to double the annual exclusion amount. One of the rules about gifts is that the person receiving it has to have the opportunity to accept it, otherwise it's something else that's not a gift, and the gift tax annual exclusion only applies to gifts. A trust with Crummey provisions is designed for you to transfer into your trust the amount of your annual gift tax exclusion, removing it from your taxable estate, and the beneficiaries of the trust have the opportunity to receive all or a portion of the gift now for a certain amount of time (usually thirty days). If they don't elect to take the gift now, then it all passes into the trust, free of estate taxes.

As you can guess, it may take a number of years for you to transfer your entire interest in a sizeable cabin estate into your trust, gifting a portion each year. Tax planning is something that is better started earlier than later.

Something to consider – you can use this strategy to transfer money into your trust, and then the trust can use some of that money to purchase a life insurance policy. And then when you die, the life insurance proceeds are not part of your taxable estate, and could be used to pay the cabin mortgage, maintenance, taxes, and expenses.

If you were to fund a trust that way, you could set up the fund as a cabin endowment where the principle stayed in the trust and the income from the principle being invested paid the cabin mortgage, maintenance, taxes, and expenses. That way, the financial aspects of the cabin would not be a burden to your family.

I mentioned at the start that there is an important exception to the rule that the property you transfer into your irrevocable trust is not part of your estate. Here is the important exception: in Minnesota, any property you transfer into an irrevocable trust (other than a special needs or supplemental needs trust) after 2005 is fair game as far as Medical Assistance is concerned. If you transfer your property into an irrevocable trust, and then need to use Medical Assistance for long-term care, you may not qualify for that care when you need it and at the same time, you won't be able to access the property to liquidate it to pay for your care.

The thing I say about Medical Assistance is that you should either plan to use it or plan to not use it. If you are going to set up an irrevocable trust, it is wise to have a long-term care insurance policy. Nowadays hybrid long-term care/life insurance policies exist, so if you don't need to use it for long-term care, there is a death benefit payout to your beneficiaries.

The Dynasty Plan

A dynasty trust is designed to hold your property for many, many generations. In order to effectively do that, it has to have creditor protection and ex-spouse protection for your beneficiaries, as well as having a conservative distribution structure.

Unlike a tax planning or asset protection trust, a dynasty trust doesn't have to start as an irrevocable trust. After you die, the trust becomes irrevocable, so during your lifetime you can retain the flexibility and control.

Not every state has the rule against perpetuities. Our neighbor, South Dakota, allows a trust to last forever. There are other states that do, as well, but South Dakota happens to be rather convenient and also has the added benefits of having no state income tax and allowing directed trusts (which I'll talk more about momentarily). If you do choose to have an out-of-state trust, you may need to hire a trustee in that state.

The dynasty strategy can be added to most trusts, but you do have to be discerning in selecting the state whose laws will apply, as there can be a wide range of differences in tax consequences and each state has variations within its trust laws, so what may work to achieve specific goals in one state may not work in another.

Traditionally, the concerns people have had with dynasty trusts is that it is difficult to have beneficiaries as trustees without strict rules on distributions, so usually it is better to have an independent trustee, who usually starts out as a family friend or advisor. It doesn't take long for the trust to outlive the family friend or advisor, and then the next best choice is a professional or corporate trustee, like a bank or a trust company. Their fees can be costly and their philosophy about trust management and discretionary distributions may or may not be aligned with your philosophy. Remember, too, that you are long gone so other than through the trust document you leave behind, there's no way for you to communicate to them about your philosophy.

People don't always like leaving decisions about handling their property in the hands of some trust officer they don't know, especially when the property is something that is emotionally significant, like a family cabin or a family business. That is why some states have made allowances for *directed trusts*.

A directed trust is one in which the duties of the trustee (like making the investment decisions, making the distribution decisions, and managing the accounts) are divided among several people or committees. For the decisions regarding the investment and controlling of the trust property, you can appoint family members or trusted advisors or a board consisting of family members and advisors, while the other aspects of the trust administration can be handled by independent fiduciaries, and of course the trustee, so as to not affect the creditor and ex-spouse protections.

Directed trusts can be made very complicated with the trustee duties spread across many people or organizations, or they can be relatively simple with only the core property investment and control aspects delegated to someone other than the trustee.

In terms of a family cabin, a directed trust can be a very good idea because you can take advantage of the creditor and ex-spouse protection for generations to come, but you can also allow your family members to make decisions about the cabin – like when/if it's time to remodel or expand the cabin, whether or not to sell that cabin and buy a new one, whether or not to purchase other property to go along with the cabin (like a boat) and whether or not to sell the cabin and use the money for another type of investment.

If you're worried about making a trust now that might not work well for your family four generations from now, a possible solution is to use a trust protector. A trust protector is an independent person who has the authority to change the trust, if needed. They would be able to decide to end the trust and distribute all the property, change the terms of the trust, veto or order trust distributions, add or remove beneficiaries (especially helpful for a special needs family member not yet born), and appoint new trustees and fiduciaries.

Minnesota's trust laws are silent as to directed trusts and trust protectors, so they aren't banned in Minnesota, but we're not sure how they would be treated by the court if a case came up involving a Minnesota-based trust using either of these tools. You can put them in, we're just not certain how the court would treat them in the case of a conflict. South Dakota (and some other states), however, have explicitly put provisions for directed trusts and trust protectors in their laws. So, if you want to take advantage of these planning tools and you want to make sure that your trust works for generations to come, it's best to set up your trust with the laws of a state like South Dakota.

Chapter 4

What's Ideal and What's Real

Asking the Right Questions and Dealing with the Real Answers

I've noticed that "Minnesota nice" goes deep in many families. People don't always want to say how it really is in their family, or that certain family members have less than ideal traits. Now is not the time to look at your family with rose colored glasses. Now is the time to put aside what's ideal, and get in touch with what is real.

I'd like to remind you that as attorneys, we are not only trained and expected to take our client confidences to our graves, but we are bound to do so by the rules of profession. Notice that I am duty bound until my grave, not until yours, so there is the possibility that I'll be carrying the confidences about your family for longer than you will. But I digress.

Your cabin plan meeting your goals and working effectively in your particular family is dependent on us working with the straight facts. Saying unpleasant straight facts out loud does not mean you condone them; it doesn't mean you agree with them; it doesn't mean that you like it that way; it doesn't mean that it's your fault that it's that way; it simply means that those are the straight facts as they exist in your family today.

I'd also like to remind you that as attorneys, we hear it all. It's highly unlikely that you are going to tell us something truly shocking. It could happen, but it's not likely. As people who hear everyone's deep dark secrets, we develop a keen sense of compassion and understanding. We won't judge you – we just need you to be real so we can get the best possible result for you and your family into the future.

That said, these are the questions you are going to want to answer in formulating a plan that will fit your family.

About Owning the Cabin

1. Who currently owns the cabin?

2. Is there currently a mortgage or mortgages on the cabin property?

3. How much is the cabin worth in relation to the rest of your assets (estate)?

4. If you are no longer living, would it be best for the cabin to be owned by one or more but not all of your family members?

5. If so, will you make adjustments to how you pass on other property or assets of your estate to compensate the non-cabin owning family members?

6. Do your family members get along or is there likely to be immediate disagreement between them if they own a cabin together?

7. Does the cabin property consist of one or more lots that could be separately owned by your family members?

8. If so, would you consider this an option?

9. If you are no longer able to use it or if you are no longer living, do you want the cabin to stay in the family?

10. What does staying in the family mean to you? Does it include in-laws? Does it include nieces and nephews?

11. Who would you not like to own the cabin?

12. If a family member were to divorce, would you want to prevent an ex-in-law from owning a share of the cabin?

13. Are there certain members of the family who definitely do not want to own the cabin? Who are they?

14. Have you talked to your family about their expectations about the cabin? If so, what have they said? Did you talk to everyone?

15. If a child of yours is not interested in owning the cabin, should your other children be able to have the first option to buy out their share?

16. If so, should they receive full price for their share or a reduced amount in order to discourage them from asking to be bought out?

17. If a family member is being bought out, what should the terms of the payments be? (down payment plus x number of payments, or payments for x number of years, etc.)

18. If you are not living, are you open to the cabin being sold?

19. Should any member of your family (or a person who is not a family member) have the first option to purchase the cabin?

20. If yes, would this be at the fair market value at the time, or at a reduced price?

21. If you were to sell the cabin during your lifetime, should any member of your family (or a person who is not a family member) have the first option to purchase the cabin?

22. If yes, would this be at the fair market value at the time, or at a reduced price?

23. Under what circumstances is it okay to sell the cabin?

24. If the cabin is sold, what happens with the proceeds of the sale?

25. Are there any potential legal issues with the cabin, like boundary disputes, neighboring development, water usage, zoning, etc.?

26. What are your primary worries about how the cabin will be owned in the future?

27. Do any of your family members have problems managing money?

28. Do any of your family members have drug or alcohol issues?

29. Are any of you family members in a troubled marriage?

About Using the Cabin

30. Are there certain members of the family that are more likely to use the cabin?

31. Are there family members who would rarely or never use the cabin?

32. Are there family members that are likely to use the cabin in a way that would bother other family members?

33. Are there any activities you would not want to ever take place at the cabin?

34. How is time spent at the time cabin allocated? By set blocks of time? On a first-schedule first-serve basis? Some other way?

35. During a family's time at the cabin, do they have exclusive use of the cabin or can others drop in?

36. Are there restrictions on bringing guests?

37. If someone doesn't want to use all their allocated time, can they give that time to another family member? Can they give that time to non-family members?

38. When and how do you want the cabin to be used:
    a. By the family as a whole?
    b. By individual members?
    c. For special holidays?

39. Do you want teenagers to be allowed to use the cabin unsupervised?

40. What are your primary worries about how the cabin time will be shared in the future?

41. What are your primary worries about how the cabin will be used in the future?

About Paying For the Cabin

42. Do you now or do you plan on using the cabin as an income generating property?

43. Do you anticipate the next generation using the cabin as an income generating property?

44. Do you have a plan for paying off the cabin mortgage upon your death?

45. If the cabin passes to your family subject to a mortgage, can they financially afford to pay it?

46. If so, do you foresee them being willing to pay it?

47. How do you want taxes, insurance, and maintenance paid for:
    a. During your lifetime?
    b. After you're gone?

48. How are other expenses (utilities, equipment, supplies) paid for:
    a. During your lifetime?
    b. After you're gone?

49. If you are no longer living, could your family members afford to pay for the routine expenses of maintaining the cabin?

50. Do you foresee any family members being unwilling to contribute?

51. If you are no longer living, could your family members afford to pay for the non-routine expenses of maintaining the cabin and improvements for the cabin? (replacing the roof, grading the access road, replacing the dock, adding air conditioning, expanding the structure)

52. Do you foresee any family members being unwilling to contribute?

53. Would you consider leaving a sum of money in your Will or buying a life insurance policy to pay for maintenance and expenses on the cabin?

54. If so, how much funding would you anticipate leaving behind?

55. If you aren't going to leave a maintenance fund behind, are your kids required to contribute for the cabin?

56. What happens if someone isn't contributing their share? Do they have a negative capital account? Does equity get reallocated? Does it trigger a first option buy-out clause?

57. Is there anyone in the family who is currently doing a majority of the maintenance or using their own money to maintain or improve the property?

58. Would you want caretaking to be compensated in some way after you're gone?

59. What are your primary worries about how the cabin will be paid for in the future?

About Managing the Cabin

60. If you are living but no longer able to make decisions concerning the cabin, is there a

family member you want to be in charge of making decisions concerning the cabin?

61. After you die, do you want management decisions to be made by all the owners or by a governing board?

62. Are there some decisions that should be made by all the owners and other decisions that could be made by a governing board?

63. If the owners or the governing board is in deadlock, is there a family member who makes the final decision?

64. If decisions are made by a governing board, how many people are on the board? How are board members selected?

65. If the cabin is managed by owners, are there circumstances where there could be non-voting owners? For example, when an in-law? When a minor? When incapacitated?

66. If owners will always vote, will there be restrictions on who can vote on behalf of a minor or incapacitated owner?

67. Is there a family member who tends to manage decisions within the family?

68. If so, do the other family members welcome their management or do they resent it?

69. Are there particular family members who are known to disagree or argue often?

70. After you are gone, is there someone that you would want to select as the point of contact for the cabin owners as to the outside world (bill collectors, service providers, etc.)?

71. If they are unwilling or unable to act as the point of contact, how will a successor person be selected?

72. What are your primary worries about how the cabin will be managed in the future?

73. Is there anything else you need to take into consideration, given your particular family? Any special needs or disabled family members? Any troubled or abusive relationships? Any family members known for causing drama?

Sometimes when families sit down to talk about these things, they find that there isn't consensus, or that what they assumed to be others' perspective was way off base. If that happens in your family, know that it is okay and that it is quite normal. It is better to get it aired out now, rather than creating a plan that occurs to your family as a burden after you're gone – or worse, a plan that creates the very thing you were seeking to avoid: conflict.

I encourage you to be open minded when talking to your family. That doesn't mean you have to agree with them, it means that you are open to listening to what they think and pausing for at least a moment to consider their point of view. Sometimes solutions present themselves in those moments of pause. What you don't want to do is make others feel like you are making them wrong for their point of view. Whatever they tell you, even if you disagree with them, thank them for sharing their thoughts and feelings.

Remember that it is difficult to tell someone something that is going to be upsetting or disappointing to them, and even more so to someone you love. If you don't give them a bit of grace and the space to say what they have to say without push-back, then they will simply tell you what you want to hear. It's human nature. What you want to hear will not help your family in the long run; dealing with what's real will.

It is your cabin and ultimately you have the final say. If you start down the path of cabin planning and find that it will not be worthwhile for your family, then it's your prerogative to do something else with the cabin. Perhaps you donate it to a charitable organization after you're gone, or perhaps you direct that it be sold, or perhaps you'll come up with an even better idea that resonates with you.

Chapter 5

Making a Plan to Keep the Peace

Choosing the Right Planning Option for Your Situation and Your Goals

Making a plan that works for your family isn't as easy as simply picking between a cabin co-ownership agreement, a cabin LLC, or a cabin trust, and then getting the documents done. If you are earnest about wanting to keep the cabin in the family and keep the peace, there's a process to go through, and then you choose which option works best for your family based on your situation and goals.

The Process of Planning

1. Have a conversation.

You would be surprised about how many people haven't talked to their kids or grandkids about their thoughts about the future of the cabin before they endeavor to make a cabin plan. While the cabin has been a wonderful haven for your family, going there regularly may not fit into your children's plan for their lifestyle, and if going there regularly doesn't work for them, then maintaining it regularly really won't work either. It's nice to know who thinks they may want to use the cabin, who would be open to managing the property, and which of your kids have no interest in it. It's better to tailor your plan to fit your family – instead of making a plan and hoping it will fit your family. You can't do that if you haven't talked with them about their expectations and yours.

2. Create a system for sharing time.

A potential hot-spot for family conflict is when everyone wants to use the cabin at the same high-demand times, like holiday weekends in the summer, and there's no system in place for fairly distributing cabin use and no system in place for decision making when potential schedule overlap happens.

3. Create a system for sharing expenses.

Another potential hot-spot for family conflict is how taxes, maintenance, and other expenses will be handled after you aren't there to foot the bill. This is often related to how the cabin is being used - the ones who are using it the most expecting that all owners contribute the same because everyone's equity in the cabin is growing at the same rate; but the ones who aren't using the cabin think they shouldn't have to pay, or think they should pay less, because they aren't getting any immediate benefit from the cabin while others are.

4. Create a system for decision making.

Even if you have created systems for sharing the cabin's use and expenses, there are still plenty of other decisions that need to be made from time to time. Is it okay for one family member to store stuff up at the cabin? Is it okay for one family member to decide to redecorate? Who decides when things like linens get replaced? What's the rule about food that's left in the cupboard? The list of questions is endless and can often be unexpected. Without a system for decision making, the family dynamics can play out in a way that has some people feeling bullied and others resenting having to deal with the situation.

5. Choose leadership wisely.

When it comes to choosing who the decision makers are going to be, whether it's a formal board or a trustee or an informal appointment of leadership, it's best to be pragmatic and not necessarily fair. It may seem pragmatic in your family to give everyone an equal say, but in many families, that's not the case. When there is deadlock among the owners, having a process for final decision making is valuable. Otherwise, people can get entrenched in their positions, sometimes to such a degree that it causes very deep family discord.

6. Make it possible for those who want out to get out.

Being an owner of a part of a cabin doesn't work for everybody. For whatever reason someone may want out, it's best if there are some rules around that – like giving the first option to buy to family members, or structuring buy-out provisions with an incremental payment structure, and even determining how the shares in the cabin should be valued. If you don't provide this and someone wants out, it's up to the family to negotiate the terms and buy them out. Otherwise the one who wants out can bring an *action for partition*, which is an expensive lawsuit that will result in the cabin being sold and then everyone is out.

7. Make it possible for those who want to stay to buy the shares.

Many people are two pay checks away from having to downgrade their lifestyle. The reality may be that your family members might not be able to finance a buy-out or come up with a lump sum payment. If you haven't put in place buy-out rules that allow for incremental payments over time, your family members may be forced to sell. For those who want to keep the cabin, there is likely a good amount of emotional investment in it, too. This can put them in a difficult bargaining position if rules about how the value of the shares will be determined haven't been established.

8. Document your systems and rules.

You've gone through the process of thinking through all the different choices and considerations, but all that forethought won't benefit your family if you don't get it down on paper.

9. Make it legally binding.

If the systems and rules you have created and documented isn't put in some legally binding format, then your family can disregard the systems and rules as soon as doing so is more convenient than following them. If you really want your planning to work when your family needs it, you need to make it legally enforceable.

10. Share the plan with your family.

Now it comes full circle. We started with a conversation with the family about what their desires and expectations were. Now the conversation is about the plan that is in place, how it works, and what to expect going forward.

Considering Your Larger Plan

Some people have their cabin succession stand on its own, completely separate from the rest of their estate planning, and other people build their cabin succession into their overall estate plan. Depending on your current plan and your overall strategy, some cabin planning tools may work better than others.

If you choose a cabin co-ownership agreement or a cabin LLC, you will need to think about how you want your share of ownership to transfer. If you want it to transfer according to your current will or trust, or if you haven't made a will or trust, according to the state's plan under the law, then you're done. If you want the cabin to pass differently than how it would be handled according to your will or trust, or the state's plan, then it's time to do an update or to create a new plan.

If you choose a cabin trust, the trust owns the cabin and you no longer have the cabin in your estate, and unlike with a cabin LLC, you don't actually "own" shares of the trust. Therefore, a cabin trust can stand alone and not affect your current estate plan, if you have made one.

Making the Right Choice

The right choice for you and your family depends on your situation and your goals. There is no one option that is empirically better than the others – if you think a cabin trust is "the best" but it doesn't match your goals, then it's not the best choice for you.

Situations

The following table has a list of common situations and the tools that are best suited for those situations. For each situation that applies to you and your family, make a circle around each "x" on that line. When you are done, add up the number of x's for that column. The columns in which the number you circled most closely matches the number possible are likely the better choices for you to consider, given your situation.

Situation	Cabin Trust	Cabin LLC	Cabin Co-Ownership Agreement
You are the sole owner of the cabin.	x	x	
You share ownership of the cabin with someone else.	x	x	x
You anticipate needing Medical Assistance in the future.		x	x
You have five or more children.	x	x	
You have fewer than five children.	x	x	x

Your children are not close, or tend to bicker when they are together.	x		
Your children and grand-children get along just fine.	x	x	x
You have a child or grandchild that has special needs (with a government recognized disability).	x		
You have a child or grandchild with alcohol or chemical dependency.	x		
You have a child or grandchild who is irresponsible with money.	x	x	
You have a child or grandchild who has a rocky marriage.	x	x	
Your cabin has appreciated in value significantly while you've owned it.	x (revocable)		x
Your cabin hasn't appreciated much in value since you've owned it, but it is likely to appreciate in the future.	x (dynasty)	x	
Total			
Out of # Possible	12	9	5

Goals

This table has a list of common goals and the tools that are best suited for those goals. For each situation that applies to you and your family, make a circle around each "x" on that line. When you are done, add up the number of x's for that column. The columns in which the number you circled most closely matches the number possible are likely the better choices for you to consider, given your goals.

Goals	Cabin Trust	Cabin LLC	Cabin Co-Ownership Agreement
You want your cabin to stay in the family for many more generations.	x (dynasty)	x	
You want to exclude in-laws from getting a share of the cabin.	x	x	
You want your children to be empowered to make decisions after you are gone.	x (directed)	x	x
You want the rules you create now to stay in place or be difficult to change.	x		
You want the rules you create now to be easily changed in the next generations.		x	x

You want to provide for the maintenance, taxes, and expenses for the cabin.	x	x	
You want to avoid having your estate go before the probate court.	x		
You want to avoid estate taxes.	x (tax)		
You want to take advantage of the generation-skipping transfer tax exemption.	x (dynasty)		
You want a leader or leaders who can make situational decisions.	x	x	
You want a management body that is different or less extensive than the owners.	x	x	
You want to provide some liability protection for the owners.	x	x	
You want to avoid having your family pay capital gains tax on the cabin.	x (revocable)		x

You want your cabin to possibly generate income, now or in the future.	x	x	
You want your cabin plan to be separate from the remainder of your estate planning.	x		
You want your cabin plan to be folded into your larger estate plan.	x	x	x
Total			
Out of # Possible	15	10	4

On balance, you'll want to look at a combination of your situation, your goals, your best options, and the tax and expense consequences of each option. In some, you may be saving on your estate tax but putting a larger capital gains tax burden on your family, or it may be that what your family saves in capital gains gets spent in the probate process. Like I've said before, no two families are alike, so no two cabin plans are alike.

When it comes time to choose which option is best for you, you'll want to crunch some numbers. Use the table on the next page to lay it all out.

Estimated costs using . . .	No Cabin Plan	Cabin Trust	Cabin LLC	Cabin Co-Ownership Agreement
Legal fees for setting up the cabin plan	■			
Other expenses for setting up the cabin plan	■			
Legal fees for action for partition (if no cabin plan)		■	■	■
Other expenses for action for partition (if no cabin plan)		■	■	■
Legal fees for probate (if probate not avoided in entire plan)				
Other expenses for probate (if probate not avoided in entire plan)				
Costs of ongoing administration of cabin plan	■			
Estate tax (if taxable estate without a tax plan)				
Capital gains tax (if transferred without a step up in basis) *For trusts, no tax if revocable trust, taxed if irrevocable trust	■			■
Total				

You may need the help of your attorney and/or CPA to get within an accurate ballpark, but doing this work will be worth it. You will know what the price of your planning will be, the costs of not doing the planning, and the value that the planning will bring your family. That's peace of mind.

Chapter 6

Getting It Done

What's Next and What to Expect

What's Next?

By the time you've reached this point, you either have done a good deal of groundwork for your plan or you are getting ready to. Cabin planning doesn't have to be hard – simply ask the questions that need to be asked of yourself and your family, register what your situation and your goals are, crunch the numbers on whether or not making your system into a legally enforceable plan is a good use of your resources, and if so, contact an estate planning lawyer familiar with this type of work to help you out. Yes, there's a good deal involved, but it doesn't have to be difficult – especially since I've given you the tools that you need to get started.

What's next is to take the ten steps I outlined in the last chapter under the process of planning. Some of those steps you will take on your own, and some of those steps you will want to take alongside the advice of legal counsel. Cabin planning, after all, does have a technical legal component; but like I've said before, that doesn't mean it has to be hard.

When looking at the scope of the ten steps, some people feel overwhelmed. Don't be. You don't have to do this all at once. That said, if you don't set some time limits for yourself, you'll lose momentum and you'll never get it done. Here is what I recommend: give yourself a year to get the whole process complete. Pick a starting point – maybe today. Then give yourself one month to complete step one. If you complete it before month's end, great! Put the date on your calendar and put reminder for yourself two weeks out.

At this point, if not sooner, you will want to start having your conversation with your attorney. He or she has seen their fair share of family situations and knows the things that can happen given differing circumstances. It would be a good time to talk over what you learned in your conversations with your family from step one and give him or her your initial thoughts about what you might want to do. They can help to provide some options and proposed solutions for creating your systems that you might not have thought about.

Steps two and three are usually integrally intertwined, so it makes sense to examine them together, although you do need to use step two as the starting place. Come up with your system for sharing time, and then start to create your system for sharing expenses. Look to see how they mesh together – given the rules of each system, are they fair (although remember that fair doesn't always mean equal)? Are they logical? Are they likely to be accepted by the family? You may need to either go back and tweak your system for sharing time or you may need to tweak your system for sharing expenses. Give yourself some time to create the systems, and then give yourself some time to mull over what you've done. I call it letting things percolate, and I find that when I do some work and then let it percolate, when I come back to it I immediately see what is good, I see what needs more work, and I see solutions I didn't see before. These two steps are the lynchpin of your cabin plan, so allow yourself to really think it through. On the calendar, give yourself two months to get these steps complete.

Like steps two and three, steps four and five are integrally intertwined. It wouldn't make sense to create a system for decision making that was unworkable given the selection of leaders that you have available. Sometimes people get stuck on this part, and this is another time when it is a good idea to have a conversation with your attorney. Give yourself two months to get this part complete, although include having follow-up conversations with your chosen leaders to make sure they are willing to serve within that time.

Steps six and seven are in tandem, and to do them you might need to have some follow-up conversations with specific members of the family to find out what they might be able to afford and/or even if they could afford a buy-out, if they would be willing to use their resources that way. You may need to look into alternative funding solutions, like life insurance, and you may need to think about updating your overall estate plan. This is another place where you may want to get some advice from your attorney. You'll want to make sure that you aren't leaving your family with some unintended consequences that you might not have thought about. Give yourself two months to get these steps done.

Step eight shouldn't take you that long since you've already done the heavy lifting (the thinking, conversing, reconsidering, and finally deciding). All you need to do now is put it all on paper in a legible format that others can understand. Give yourself a month for this, although really you just need an afternoon.

Step nine is a bit out of your control. For more about why that may be, you could skip ahead to the section called How Much Time Is This Going to Take? Although it may sound like a lot of time now, give yourself three months for this on your time-line. If it gets complete sooner, great!

Step ten completes the circle. You may not need as much time for this step as you did for step one because you have one final plan to present to your family, instead of asking a lot of questions and getting everyone's ideas. If your family is such that you can bring everyone together to unveil and talk through your cabin plan, you may not need much time at all. If not, you may be having the same or similar conversation multiple times. Give yourself a month to get this step complete, and that rounds out your year.

About Choosing your Attorney

According to the American Bar Association, there are approximately 25,000 attorneys in Minnesota. Of course, not all of them do estate planning. Of the attorneys that do estate planning, not all of them do advanced estate planning (like tax planning or dynasty trusts), and even fewer still do cabin planning. Why? Because they aren't your run-of-the-mill sort of thing, they require a lot more time talking through the details of how it's going to work, and the relationship dynamics are often much more involved. Attorneys who do cabin planning also do advanced estate planning, but the opposite isn't always the case.

Take heart! The attorneys who actually do cabin planning regularly do so because they like making plans that are not run-of-the-mill, they like helping people navigate the details of their individual plan, and they like getting to know their clients on a more personal level.

What you want to look for in an attorney is someone who fits the description in the above paragraph and who likes to maintain life-long relationships with their clients. It's difficult to do a cabin plan with one attorney, and then have some circumstance happen that makes a change in your plan a good idea, and then have to start from scratch with someone new who doesn't already understand your family's particular situation.

It's much better, too, to work with someone who wants to stay connected to you so that as your circumstances change, they can advise you when something needs to be updated and when the plan is just fine as it is. What you don't want is someone who thinks of your plan as a document to draft, rather than thinking of you as a person to have a relationship with.

So, How Much Is All This Going to Cost?

Which planning tool is right for you and your family, your situation, and your goals will be one factor in the cost of the planning. Another factor will be whether or not you have other planning that needs to happen for the remainder of your estate. Yet another factor will be the attorney that you choose. When it comes to the attorney you choose, how they charge can be just as important as how much they charge.

Some attorneys charge by the hour, and they may or may not be able to tell you how long your particular plan will take to complete. Fair enough; it may take your family twice as long to figure it all out than the family down the road. It's been my experience, though, that people hate it when they are told that it's going to cost several hundred dollars per hour and there's no telling how long it will really take. It's what has people not want to call their attorney when they have questions and concerns; it's what has people not want to update their plan when they think (or even know) they need to.

Since people hate hourly billing rates, hate uncertain final costs, and hate watching the clock tick away, many attorneys have gone to flat-fee billing for things like estate planning. People love that – they know exactly how much it is going to cost from the start, they know there aren't going to be any surprises later, and they are at ease in working with their attorney. You might think that attorneys would like it less than billing by the hour, but my experience is the opposite. The attorney knows that what they are charging is a fair value for the service and because the clients are at ease, communication is better and more frequent; and with better communication, the attorney can produce better results with less stress. Really, everybody wins.

Whether or not you choose an attorney who charges by the hour or on a flat-fee basis, the details of how you are paying and when should be detailed in a client agreement, or at the very least, in an engagement letter. While you don't have to have these details in writing for estate planning, it's a good idea to have something to fall back on if any questions arise.

How Long Is This Going to Take?

How long your cabin plan takes to get completed depends on two factors: 1) you (and your family) and 2) how busy your lawyer is at the moment. From start to finish, cabin planning can take a good amount of time. I don't mean that it takes hours and hours on end; I mean that the days can turn into weeks, weeks into months, while a lot of smaller conversations are had and while certain details are on hold for decisions to be made.

Cabin plans can be rather detailed and a good plan is customized to fit your family's particular situation and goals. What that means is that your attorney is going to need some time to assimilate all your information, think it through, document it in a way that is efficient and effective, review it for inconsistencies and omissions, and then prepare it to be finalized and executed.

Sometimes families take months to pull together all the information they need to get to their attorney, and then expect their attorney to complete the plan in a very short amount of time. Sometimes they say,

"Our cabin plan has taken eight months; it's taking too long! When will this ever get complete?", when seven and a half months were spent with the attorney waiting on information from the client. When you work with your attorney, please be courteous and give them the time they need to do a very good job creating your plan once all your information is submitted. And remember, their plate may be full right when they get the last pieces of information they need, so your plan will be the next thing scheduled to be worked on, but that might not be immediately.

That said, it's reasonable to ask your attorney when the plan can be ready for finalization, and then expect that it will be complete in that time frame. You and your attorney should be able to communicate about that progress and each of your respective time expectations.

My Final Words

How much it costs and how long it takes to do this planning is really the least of your worries. Consider instead the cost to your family in relationship conflict if you don't get around to getting this planning done before you're gone. Consider the monetary cost to your family in dealing with the legal aspects of the property if you don't get around to getting this planning done before you're gone. I promise you the price is much lower now, and the value is much higher, too.

By the way, if you think this planning sounds expensive, you are right and you are wrong. I can guarantee you that it is substantially less costly than it would be for your family to fight over the cabin after you're gone, and I've never had a family who believed in the value of this important planning to leave my office because they couldn't afford it. We've made monthly payment plans available because we know this planning is the foundation for peace in your family for generations to come.

I'd love to see if we could help your family, too.

About the Author

I am not your typical lawyer. First of all, I don't have the mindset of the typical lawyer, and I certainly haven't had the usual career path. I came to my legal career after being a fashion designer in New York and moving away for family reasons. It's hard to be a fashion designer anywhere else, it really is.

After I became a lawyer, I started my practice and started practicing just like every other lawyer I know practices. As I was going along, I kept noticing that most law practices violate the laws of good business (and clients hate that but lawyers continue that way nonetheless). Laws of good business like providing a good experience for the client (more than just a good result), like building relationships with clients (and not just a merry-go-round of new prospects), and providing a level of care that is personalized and focused on what is important to the client (and not calling all the shots like we know what is best for you). It is amazing that law practices succeed given the usual practice model, and it is no wonder that people hate lawyers.

I don't want to be the lawyer that people hate. I want to be the lawyer that people love.

As my practice grew, I stepped further and further away from the typical law model. I stopped doing divorce work. I stopped doing whatever-came-in-the-door work. I started focusing on what I could do that made a positive difference for people, that had me enjoy my practice and my clients, and that contributed to society. I stopped billing by the hour. I started running my law practice based on relationship principles. It has been a progression, and I'm constantly working to improve upon it, but I love how my law practice is now. I love my clients. I love my work. It's fun being a lawyer – the way I'm doing it.

My favorite part of what I do is working with people. I think it is a profound privilege to get to do what I do. I see things differently than most lawyers, and once people realize that about me, they really appreciate that difference.

Nonetheless, you may still want to know all about my credentials and such, so here they are. I graduated with honors from the University of Tulsa College of Law in May 2008, where I also received a certificate in Native American Law and a certificate in International and Comparative Law. I served as an editor on the Tulsa Journal of Comparative and International Law and I had a scholarly legal article published in that journal. I am licensed in Oklahoma, Minnesota, and the US District Court for the District of Minnesota.

I also serve on the Board of Directors for Empowering Adults Protecting Children, a non-profit organization whose mission is to educate people how to recognize behaviors in adults that are a risk to children and intervene in non-threatening ways. I also serve on the Advisory Board for Family Innocence, a non-profit organization whose mission is to provide an alternative to family court for families in conflict. I also serve as a volunteer Ambassador for Guild, Inc., a non-profit organization that serves mentally ill adults in the community. I also serve on the Development Committee for East Side Neighborhood Services, a non-profit human services organization that provides a wide array of services to low income individuals and families. I've been an integral part of developing the organization's legacy program and I helped implement the Elder Legal Clinic that provides pro-bono legal advice and estate planning to seniors in the community. It's some of the most rewarding work I do.

I also co-own MoreLaw Minneapolis, an executive suite exclusively for attorneys, with my mother, Sara. My office is located within that suite and I'll be delighted to give you the nickel tour if we have an appointment together. I enjoy growing that business and it's rewarding to get to help other attorneys to succeed. I love the community that we've built. In May 2013, I was awarded a Women in Business Award by the Minneapolis St. Paul Business Journal for my work with MoreLaw Minneapolis and for my commitment to the larger Twin Cities community.

Believe it or not, before going to law school, I was a fashion designer in New York City. And no, I don't watch Project Runway, although the one episode I did see reminded me of final exam time in my fashion design program in college. I earned my Bachelor's degree from the Fashion Institute of Technology (State University of New York) in New York City in Apparel Production Management in 1998 and I earned an Associate's degree from that same school in Fashion Design in 1995. I worked as a fashion designer in the apparel industry until I moved back to Oklahoma for family reasons.

Sometimes people ask me if I miss New York, or if I miss the fashion industry. I like New York, but I don't miss it. I love the Twin Cities and I find that the work I do now is infinitely more fulfilling to me. At the end of the day, making a difference for someone with something that is important to them is much more satisfying. I have come to understand that the path to happiness lies in serving others.

In my free time, I still enjoy creating artwork and I like exploring Minneapolis' vibrant arts community. I've had the privilege to befriend and know artist Jason Najarak and paint with him, just as he knew Pablo Picasso and painted with him. I also love traveling and exploring new places, and I always enjoy meeting people and experiencing different cultures. I consider myself a lifetime learner, and I love to read and study topics that enrich my life and the lives of the people around me.

Would you like to contact me? I'd love to hear from you.

Kimberly M. Hanlon
Kimberly M. Hanlon, LLC
310 4th Avenue South, Suite 5010
Minneapolis, Minnesota 55415
kimberly@khanlonlaw.com
www.khanlonlaw.com
www.minnesotacabinplanning.com

CPSIA information can be obtained at www.ICGtesting.com
Printed in the USA
LVOW08s2033100515

437954LV00001B/2/P